CW00833237

SEVEN WHOLE DAYS

Finding God in everyday life

Tom Carson and Raymond Tomkinson

kevin
mayhew

www.kevinmayhew.com

kevin mayhew

First published in Great Britain in 2015 by Kevin Mayhew Ltd
Buxhall, Stowmarket, Suffolk IP14 3BW
Tel: +44 (0) 1449 737978 Fax: +44 (0) 1449 737834
E-mail: info@kevinmayhew.com

www.kevinmayhew.com

© Copyright 2015 Tom Carson and Raymond Tomkinson.

The rights of Tom Carson and Raymond Tomkinson to be identified as the authors
of this work has been asserted by them in accordance with the Copyright, Designs
and Patents Act 1988.

The publishers wish to thank all those who have given their permission to
reproduce copyright material in this publication.

Every effort has been made to trace the owners of copyright material and we hope
that no copyright has been infringed. Pardon is sought and apology made if the
contrary be the case, and a correction will be made in any reprint of this book.

All rights reserved. No part of this publication may be reproduced, stored in
a retrieval system, or transmitted, in any form or by any means, electronic,
mechanical, photocopying, recording, or otherwise, without the prior written
permission of the publisher.

Unless stated otherwise, Scripture quotations are taken from *The New Revised
Standard Version Bible: Anglicized Edition*, copyright © 1989, 1995, Division of
Christian Education of the National Council of the Churches of Christ in the
United States of America. Used by permission. All rights reserved.

9 8 7 6 5 4 3 2 1 0

ISBN 978 1 84867 822 4
Catalogue No. 1501509

Cover design by Justin Minns
© Images used under licence from Shutterstock Inc.
Edited by Virginia Rounding
Typeset by Melody-Anne Lee

Printed and bound in Great Britain

Contents

Acknowledgements   5

About the authors   7

Introduction   9

Sunday   15

Monday   23

Tuesday   33

Wednesday   45

Thursday   55

Friday   63

Saturday   73

For all those whose daily walk with the Lord
has inspired us.

Acknowledgements

First and foremost, my deepest thanks to Raymond for the privilege of co-writing this book with you. Your wisdom as a spiritual director and friend has made it a wonderful experience. Thank you for believing in me as an author. Thanks to the people of the parish of the Mortlake with East Sheen Team Ministry for the joy of ministering to them, many of whom have heard bits and pieces of this material before. Thanks are also due to my cell group, Annie, Christopher and Ali, for all of their encouragement which helps me to 'keep on keeping on'. My gratitude to all of my family, especially my dad who first introduced me to the idea that we should try to live 'seven whole days' as Christians. Finally, thanks to my wife, Marian, for her loving support for all I do.

Tom

It has been a pleasure to work with Tom on this book. His deep faith, fresh insights, energy, enthusiasm and attention to detail have been life-giving. I am grateful, also, to those whose daily discipleship has inspired the stories which serve to illustrate the themes in this book. As ever, thanks are due to my dear wife, Rose, for her loving support and generosity in ensuring I have time and space to write.

Raymond

We would both like to thank the Revd David Cowie for his helpful insights into the development of the ancient canonical hours into contemporary 'daily office' liturgies and their influence, as a spiritual discipline, on the deepening of the spiritual life. Our thanks are due, too, to Virginia Rounding for her patient editing and to all the team at Kevin Mayhew Limited.

About the authors

Before being ordained as a priest in the Church of England, Tom Carson was a secondary school teacher and Head of Religious Education at a school in Wallington. Having served as Assistant Curate in the Mortlake with East Sheen Team Ministry in the Diocese of Southwark, he now works as Chaplain of Exeter School in Devon. He has a Master of Arts in Philosophy and Religion from Heythrop College, London, and a Master's in Applied Theology from Oxford University. Tom is married to Marian and has two children, Zoe and Barney. In addition to writing, Tom enjoys running half marathons, walking in the country and cookery.

Raymond Tomkinson spent some time in religious life before becoming a State Registered Nurse specialising in the care of elderly people and in hospice care. He was a hospital manager and staff development officer before training for ordained ministry. He has been a parish priest and area dean in the Church of England and has also held vocations adviser and clergy development posts. He was director of a diocesan retreat centre until 2006. In 2005 he began working at Ripon College Cuddesdon, an Anglican theological college and seminary near Oxford. Following four years serving as a visiting spiritual director, he went on to serve for five years as College Chaplain with some teaching responsibilities in the field of Christian spirituality. In 2010 he was awarded a Master's degree in Ministry (Distinction) by Oxford Brookes University. He continues to be sought out for spiritual direction and to lead quiet days and retreats. Raymond lives in Rutland with his wife, Rose, near their daughter and her family.

Other works by Raymond Tomkinson published by Kevin Mayhew include *Come to me . . .* (2000), *God's Good Fruit* (2002), *God's Advent People* (2003), *Clothed in Christ* (2008), *Hard Time Praying?* (2009), *Life Shaping Spirituality* (2014) and *Called to Greatness: Reflections on Vocation and Ambition in the Church* (2015). He is a contributor to *Sermons on Difficult Subjects* (2011) and *Services for Special Occasions* (2012). Other works include *Called to Love: Discernment, Decision-Making and Ministry*, published by SCM Press in 2012.

Introduction

In the hymn 'King of Glory, King of Peace', George Herbert, the sixteenth-century poet priest, prayerfully exclaims: 'Sev'n whole days, not one in sev'n, I will praise thee'.[1] It often feels to many of us in an ordinary week as though we don't even manage to praise God for seven whole minutes! Yet God is calling us to engage with him 'seven whole days' of every week. More than that, God calls us into friendship with him. He is calling us into a 24-hour relationship each day, in which he is involved in every aspect of our lives, even those parts we might not think of as being remotely spiritual. Many of us can find, however, that while we may meet with God at church it's all too easy to neglect that relationship after Sunday worship, only to pick it up again a week later at the next Sunday service. How should our faith and our relationship with God in prayer impact the rest of our week? Here we explore how we might take a sense of God's presence into our normal lives, into our everyday routines, into those activities which may not feel especially sacred, like catching a bus or going to sleep at night. The question we ask throughout is: 'where can we find God today?'

When we begin to believe that we can find God everywhere and in everything, we find ourselves doing what Christian spiritual tradition calls the practice of the presence of God.

---

1. *Complete Anglican Hymns Old and New* (Kevin Mayhew Ltd, 2000), No.375.

The approach we take in this book is influenced by the writings of Brother Lawrence of the Resurrection (1611-1691). He was an uneducated lay cook in a French monastery who lived more than 300 years ago and who discovered how to enjoy a profound awareness of God moment by moment, even in the midst of busyness and distraction. Though he spent most of his time working in the kitchens, he tried to practise the presence of God in all things. 'The time of business,' he said, 'does not with me differ from the time of prayer. In the noise and clatter of my kitchen, while several persons are at the same time calling for different things, I possess God in as great a tranquillity as if I were upon my knees at the Blessed Supper.'[2]

How did Brother Lawrence achieve this? His writings, and reports of conversations with him, suggest three aspects. Firstly, he firmly believed that God is close to us, far closer than we are aware of. In order for us to start practising the presence of God, 'we need only to recognise God intimately present to us'.[3]

Secondly, he tried to give himself a sense that God was with him always by talking with him. Lawrence suggests speaking to God 'frankly and plainly, imploring His assistance in our affairs, just as they happen'.[4] In fact, he explicitly says that 'it is not necessary for being with God to be always at church'

---

2. Brother Lawrence, *The Practice of the Presence of God and The Spiritual Maxims* (Dover Publications, 2005), p.16.
3. Brother Lawrence, p.12.
4. Brother Lawrence, p.8.

but rather we can 'make an oratory of our heart wherein to retire from time to time to converse with Him in meekness, humility and love'.[5] He later notes that everyone is capable of this kind of dialogue with God. We're sure he would add that our faster-paced world today need make no difference. The more we attend on God, the more natural it will seem to us and will gradually become habitual.

Thirdly, whatever task Brother Lawrence was doing he tried to think of himself as being about 'God's business'. He tried to make the love of God the *end* of all his actions. For Brother Lawrence, we don't need to change the content of what we're doing to become holy. Instead, we should do 'for God's sake' that which 'we commonly do for our own'. It all depends on *who* we're working for; for Lawrence it shouldn't be either for others or for ourselves, but rather for God. He is reported to have said 'that the most excellent method he had found of going to God, was that of doing our common business without any view of pleasing men, and (as far as we are capable) purely for the love of God'.[6]

We find Lawrence's approach particularly attractive because you don't need to *do* anything special. You don't need to *be* anyone brilliant. You don't need to go anywhere different to find God. God is already with us; we just need to notice him!

---

5. Brother Lawrence, p.29.
6. Brother Lawrence, p.13.

Prayer is the mutual expression of our relationship with God. It is never a one-sided thing. Even as God gazes on us, we gaze on God. As we speak to God, he listens to us. As God speaks to us, we listen with the ears of our heart. We speak of letting God catch our eye or of glancing in God's direction. This deep interconnectedness is how love works. God is love and mutual interconnectedness is what nourishes any loving relationship. Do we love those who are special in our lives just one day a week? Of course not! We love them seven whole days of the week. In this book we offer suggestions for nourishing and sustaining our relationship with God every day and throughout the day.

Each section of the book is dedicated to one of the seven days of the week, with just a hint of the mood attributed to some days of the week in traditional liturgical practice. Thursday, for example, reminds us of the glorious Ascension of our Lord, whereas Friday has a little hint of penitence. In each of the daily sections we suggest a text from Holy Scripture which might provide a thought for the day. Following a brief introduction, the section continues with a short story about someone encountering God in everyday life. This is followed by a reflection based on the story and includes ideas as to how Christian traditions might aid us as we seek to connect with God. The reflection is followed by suggestions for prayer and questions for individuals or groups to consider.

In order to encourage the reader to connect with God at different times of the day, each section focuses on a particular time, drawing on the ancient practice and experience of the 'hours' of prayer: Lauds, Prime, Terce, Sext, None, Vespers and Compline.

In the sixteenth chapter of his Rule, St Benedict of Nursia (c.480–543 or 547) is very specific about the praying of the daily office:

> The Prophet says: *Seven times a day have I praised you* (Ps 119:164). We will fulfil this sacred number of seven if we satisfy our obligations of service at Lauds, Prime, Terce, Sext, None, Vespers and Compline, for it was of these hours during the day that he said: Seven times a day have I praised you (Ps 119:164). Concerning Vigils, the same Prophet says: *At midnight I arose to give you praise* (Ps 119:62). Therefore, we should *praise* our Creator *for his just judgements* at these times: Lauds, Prime, Terce, Sext, None, Vespers and Compline; and *let us arise at night to give* him *praise* (Ps 119:164,62).[7]

We are not suggesting that everyone is able to respond to the scriptural injunction to 'pray without ceasing' by

---

7. *The Rule of St. Benedict in English* (RB), ed. Timothy Fry OSB (The Liturgical Press, 1981), RB 16.

engaging with a full liturgical 'office' seven times a day! Attending on the presence of God and offering up a brief but heartfelt prayer at different times of the day or night may be more manageable.

Incorporated into each section are thumbnail sketches of prayer traditions that Christians around the world have found helpful in their daily discipleship. We draw on the spirituality of St Benedict, St Ignatius of Loyola and others as well as other spiritual practices of vocal, mental and contemplative prayer.

This book could be used by individuals for the development of their own relationship with God, and the material would also provide frameworks for prayer for each day and for each part of the day: a convenient prayer book.

As implied above, this book might also be used by groups meeting regularly to work through the material: sharing experiences of the joys and challenges of meeting God over 'seven whole days' of the week and not just 'one in seven'. There are suggestions for group activities at the end of each section.

Sunday

'Early on the first day of the week, while it was still dark, Mary Magdalene came to the tomb and saw that the stone had been removed from the tomb . . . [She] went and announced to the disciples, "I have seen the Lord".'

John 20:1, 18

Sunday is the day of the resurrection of Christ: the Lord's Day. Traditionally as Christians we gather on a Sunday to worship God, seeking to nourish ourselves to live as Christians in the world in the week ahead. In this first session we explore some of the joys which Sunday might bring, and how this day prepares us to love and to encounter God through 'seven whole days'.

Chris and Julie's story

Chris popped his head round the kitchen door and asked Julie: 'Any chance of a sandwich?' They both laughed, even as Julie threw an orange at him. Truth to tell, they had spent most of that day either preparing food or clearing up after food had been eaten. Unfortunately they had eaten very little themselves. Nevertheless, it had been a wonderful day with many blessings. Their local church had held its annual Harvest Festival Eucharist service that morning, and Chris and Julie had been up early preparing food both for a children's party which took place during part of the church service and for a 'Harvest Lunch' in the church hall to which many local elderly people had been invited. Somewhere in between they had washed, dressed and fed their own three children and had managed a late afternoon visit to Grandma, whose birthday it had been. The cake they had made was nearly a disaster but, smothered in chocolate ganache, it looked fine and was much appreciated.

It was late now and Julie was getting together the makings of packed lunches for the following day. 'Leave that to me, Julie,' insisted Chris. 'You've done more than enough today. Go and put your feet up.' 'OK,' said Julie, 'but I must just sort out school uniforms, and Ben's shoes need a polish.' 'I'll do it. Go!'

Chris was tired but in a good mood as he put spread to bread. He found himself singing a chorus they had sung at the service: 'This is the day. This is the day that the Lord has made . . . We will rejoice . . . We will rejoice and be glad in it.' A tired voice from an adjacent room shouted: 'Oh Chris, please.' 'Sorry, Julie.'

As he finished putting together the packed lunches he reflected on the day: the worship, the fellowship, the washing up (ugh!). He thanked God for everything, but especially for the resurrection of Jesus, encountered that day in so many ways, for the hope it brings and for the deliciousness of the life it promises – and (as he licked his fingers) even for sandwich spread!

Pause for thought

What is your experience of Sunday?

Reflection

On Sunday Christians around the world come to worship in church, seeking to meet God. We look for him in fellowship with others, in the words of the Scriptures, in the preaching, and in the bread and wine of Holy Communion. We try to give God our focused attention, asking him to feed us for all that lies ahead of us in the coming week.

In Jesus' day worship took place on a Saturday, the Sabbath, which was the last day of the week (the day of rest). After Jesus' resurrection, however, Christians started to meet on the *first* day of the week in order to mark the day on which he rose from the dead. That is why they called it 'the Lord's Day': every Sunday is a celebration and reminder of the day of Christ's resurrection, the first day of God's new creation.

Sunday provides us with a chance to look ahead to God's new creation, to reflect upon the world as God intends it to be. Like Chris and Julie, we can encounter the hope that Jesus' resurrection brings in so many different ways. When we listen for the Word of God in the Scriptures and the sermon, we endeavour to attend to what God is saying to us today. In greeting others in 'the peace' and over refreshments, we catch a glimpse of the fellowship which God intends for humanity. As we gather around the Lord's table to share the bread and wine, we anticipate the banquet we will all share in God's kingdom.

Many communion services conclude with a prayer that God will send us out empowered by the Holy Spirit to live out our lives to God's praise and glory. We are dismissed with a commission to go out from church and to order our lives in the light and strength of the communion we have just shared. As Chris and Julie find, Sunday is often the day on which we prepare ourselves for all the coming week will hold. On Sunday we're sent out into the ordinary week to love God and to love our neighbours. Like Mary Magdalene, we've met with the Risen Lord, and now we're sent out into the world to serve him and share his good news.

One of the key ways in which we serve Christ in everyday life is through loving others. The day-in day-out reality is where the command to 'love our neighbours as ourselves' is put to the test. This is often where we may encounter challenging people who don't share our values and beliefs. Christ calls us to love *them*! In his Rule, St Benedict tried to help his followers to see that, in meeting the needs of others, they were in fact caring for Christ. He said that all guests who arrived at a monastery were 'to be welcomed as Christ'[8] and that 'Christ is to be adored because he is indeed welcomed in them'.[9] How would it change the way we behaved towards others if we regarded all the people we encountered as though they were Christ?

Perhaps one of the key things we can do on a Sunday is bring to God all the people we will be meeting throughout the week. We can hold them in prayer before God, asking him to help us love them. It may be that we ask him to help

8. RB 53.1.
9. RB 53.6.

us see them as *he* sees them, and to give us the strength to serve them as opportunities arise.

Weekdays are where we put our faith into action; they are the place where we endeavour to live out all that we've proclaimed on a Sunday. The day itself is a reminder that faith needs to be lived out through 'seven whole days'.

Questions for personal reflection or group discussion

- What is your experience of going to church?

- Does going to church on a Sunday prepare you for the coming week? If so, how?

- Are there people you find difficult to love? How could you ask God to help you?

Suggested group activity

As a group make a list of the key reasons why it is good for Christians to meet together on a Sunday (for example, to receive Holy Communion, to enjoy fellowship with other Christians, to praise God, to intercede for the needs of the world). Then try to sequence them in order of importance. Finally, discuss which of these could be left out, if any, and which are essential.

Suggestions for prayer

Lord, thank you for those 'Sunday moments':
the times when I can hear your Word clearly,
when I feel as though I've met with your Son,
when I get a glimpse of your kingdom in fellowship
with others.
Help me to take those moments with me into the rest of life
and to look for signs of your presence in the face of every
person I meet,
with the help of Jesus Christ.
Amen.

A prayer for the first day of the week

Bless us, Lord,
as we begin this new week.
Make us always mindful of the new life you have given us
through the resurrection of your dear Son, Jesus,
and help us to live joyfully and gratefully for you,
seven whole days and not just one in seven.
Amen.

Monday

'Rejoice in the Lord always; again I will say, Rejoice. Let your gentleness be known to everyone. The Lord is near. Do not worry about anything, but in everything by prayer and supplication with thanksgiving let your requests be made known to God. And the peace of God, which surpasses all understanding, will guard your hearts and your minds in Christ Jesus.'

Philippians 4:4-7

What is the first thing that comes into your head when you wake up in the morning? It is probably not: 'Praise God: it's a great new day!' Many of us are likely to wake up lamenting the fact that we haven't had enough sleep (as usual), our mind instantly buzzing with all of the tasks ahead, and wishing that we could turn over and slip back into unconsciousness . . .

We all have different life situations, but mornings for most of us can be really pressured times. There may be animals to feed or walk, children to clothe and drop off, trains to catch, emails to get on top of . . . and we have to fit breakfast in there somewhere, too! In particular, Monday mornings can be a real low point. Do you ever get that 'Monday morning feeling'? Monday arrives after a lovely weekend and it's 'back down to reality with a bump'!

How can we find God in all of this? How can we start the day well with our loving Creator? We are often so busy and stressed out in the mornings that any high-minded notions we may have had on a Sunday can easily go out the window.

Brenda's story

Brenda sings. Brenda sings everywhere: in the shower, in the subway, in the fine offices she cleans early in the morning. It was still dark that Monday morning when Brenda stood at the bus stop waiting for the number 42 to take her up west to her job, but as she waited a thin ribbon of light began to slip around the tenements, bringing the hope of a bright morning. Brenda began to hum a chorus the worship group had led the day before.

One of her neighbours joined her at the bus stop and remarked how cheerful Brenda was for so early in the morning. Brenda laughed and remarked that she was cheerful because this was a new day and Lord knows what blessings it might bring. 'Was that "prayin'" you was doin', Bren?' 'Oh, I was just singing, but Pastor says "to sing is to pray twice". He did say who first said that but I forget.[10] Look at that sky,' Brenda said, 'don't it just wanna make you sing and thank God for the beautiful world he made?' The neighbour looked doubtful. All she could see was the crumbling tenement and the litter on the street. All she could hear was the sound of the traffic beginning to build up as the Monday morning rush hour got under way.

The bus came and they both boarded. They chatted about this and that; mints were shared. Brenda's cheerfulness and optimism were so infectious. Regular commuters knew her cheerful greetings and her laughter. Brenda didn't make a big thing of her religion. She loved the Lord Jesus and she praised at the drop of a hat. Other travellers knew the source of her joy. Some may have envied it, others might have found it a bit annoying, but most shared it, borrowing it for the duration of the journey. Somehow it made the day ahead less daunting. Brenda, like joy, comes in the morning!

---

10. St Augustine of Hippo (354–430) is often quoted as having said 'He who sings, prays twice.' The Latin cited for this is '*Qui bene cantat bis orat*' or 'He who sings *well* prays twice.'

Pause for thought

How do you react to Brenda's joyful approach to mornings?

Reflection

Perhaps the most important step towards finding God in the mornings is to try to begin the day with praise. Let's face it: most of us, realistically, aren't going to get enough sleep every night; we are going to wake up with our minds buzzing, and wishing that it was a Saturday. But surely, most of us can find *something* to praise God for: perhaps the life of the new day, the sleep we *have* had, the good things we're looking forward to. We may not all have the particularly distinctive style we see in Brenda, but we can all look for reasons to be joyful rather than gloomy.

The psalms are full of the idea that we should make praising God with joy a discipline in the morning: 'Awake, my soul!' says the psalmist, 'Awake, O harp and lyre! I will awake the dawn. I will give you thanks to you, O Lord, among the peoples' (Psalm 57:8-9). Psalm 59 is a plea for rescue from enemies, but the psalmist still says, 'But I will sing of your might; I will sing aloud of your steadfast love in the morning' (Psalm 59:16). And the office of Morning Prayer (based on the ancient offices of Lauds and Prime) begins each day with some words from Psalm 51: 'O Lord, open my lips, and my mouth will declare your praise' (Psalm 51:15).

St Paul tells the Philippians to 'rejoice in the Lord always'. *Always?!* We might want to respond: 'Come off it, Paul – we can't possibly rejoice in the Lord always!' Some of us may find it hard enough trying to rejoice in the Lord for a single minute, let alone *always*. Rejoicing does not necessarily come easily to most of us, especially in the morning. It needs to be worked at. We don't always feel in the mood to be joyful, and so we need to make the effort to find things to praise God for. Paul gives us a helpful clue as to how we might do this when he writes: 'with thanksgiving'.

The regular expression of *gratitude* can lead naturally to praise. Psychological studies have found that grateful people often experience more positive emotion and higher life satisfaction, whilst those who are less grateful tend to experience lower negative emotions such as depression, anxiety and envy. What's more, they suggest that grateful people are more likely to feel empathy, to forgive, and to be more supportive in their relationships, whilst being less concerned about material possessions.

Some people have found that writing a journal helps them to reflect on how life has been during a particular period. It is easy enough to write about things that have been irritating, annoying or hurtful but it takes a bit more discipline to write down details of things for which one is grateful. There is always that little concern that someone might read one's journal so there is a temptation to be 'polite' about recent events. Having said that, the very concern about another reading the journal can be an incentive to write down positive things. After all, no one wants posterity to think that they were always grumbling and bemoaning their lot! Again, psychological studies support the idea that writing positive things (things one is grateful for or which have stirred positive and life-giving emotions in us) does tend to make us generally more grateful and positive about our life. Journaling does not suit everyone but it is a known therapeutic tool as well as a useful way to look back to see how far the Lord has brought us!

So the familiar instruction to 'count our blessings' may well genuinely make us feel more like rejoicing in the Lord. Giving God thanks doesn't even need to be all that profound. We can all find the smallest things to be grateful for: a warm cup of coffee, the smile of a friend, the sun on our face for a few moments, fresh water from our taps, the transport which takes us to work, the shelter we've enjoyed overnight. Like Brenda, we can all try to look at the sky and thank God for the beauty of the world, rather than focusing on the crumbling tenement and the litter on the street.

Jesus tells his disciples that to enter the kingdom of God we must receive it like little children (Mark 10:13-16). Being around small children can be tremendously good for us spiritually. Children don't take the world for granted; they see everything with the eyes of surprise and wonder. It's all new for them, and they want to ask questions about everything. Going for a walk with a toddler, for example, can take longer than walking with an adult because toddlers wonder about every stick, every stone, every insect. Where have we adults lost our sense of wonder? The problem may be that we stop seeing life as an amazing gift and we take our existence for granted. If we try to approach each day with the excitement of little children, we may just find that rejoicing in the Lord becomes easier.

Questions for personal reflection or group discussion

- What particular challenges do you face each morning which make praising God difficult? What could you do to remind yourself to praise God in the morning?

- Is it realistic to rejoice in the Lord always? *Always?!*

- What are some of the things you take for granted every day which you could be more grateful for?

Suggested group activities

- Try singing a children's praise song with actions together (with a sense of irony, if you need to!) and then discuss how it made you feel. Did it lift your spirits to praise God in a childlike way?

- As a group play a variation on 'I went to the shop and bought . . . ' with 'I woke up in the morning and I was grateful for . . . ' until you run out of things to be grateful for – or you can't remember the long list.

Suggestions for prayer

Lord, I've got the Monday morning feeling.
I'm back to reality with a bump!
Help me to find some joy,
to notice something to say 'thanks' for,
even if it's only the shoes on my feet.
For the sake of your Son, Jesus Christ.
Amen.

A prayer for early morning (the hour of Prime, the first hour of the day)

God of the dawning,
you dismiss the amber lights of urban streets
and the demanding glare of neon signing
with the gentle rising of the blessed Sun.
Melt into our mornings with the light of your love
made known to us in Jesus Christ our Lord.
Amen.

Tuesday

'In the morning . . . [Jesus] got up and went out to a deserted place, and there he prayed.'

Mark 1:35

Here we continue to reflect on how we might connect with God as the morning unfolds.

Mike's story

Mike had a dilemma. If he caught the 7.38am train he arrived at work 20 minutes early. If he caught the 7.58am he would arrive at work on time, provided the train was not late. His family time was precious to him so he would rather have caught the later train, but he had seen colleagues dismissed for poor time-keeping and so, reluctantly, he tended to catch the earlier train.

One Tuesday morning he was sitting at his desk waiting to begin work. He couldn't do very much as most of his job involved making telephone calls, and clients, or potential clients, did not welcome calls before 9am. He tidied his desk and opened his diary to scan his appointments for the day ahead.

Mike's desk diary was a Christmas gift from a colleague. It was very like any other diary except that, at the top of each page, was a quotation from the Bible. His colleague was very religious. She went to church every Sunday (and seemed to spend half the week there, too!). Mike was a Christian and went to church with his wife and family . . . but *every* Sunday? Getting the kids to football or drama classes cut across church service times, but they did their best. They were there last Sunday and it was OK. There was a visiting preacher who talked about stress and anxiety: how Jesus understands the pressures people are under but asks them to trust him to see them through.

Mike's diary entry reminded him that, later that morning, he was due at a team meeting with the boss. He had written: 'Forward planning'. Just above that entry was the biblical quotation for the day. It ran: 'Cast all your anxiety on him, because he cares for you' (1 Peter 5:7).

Mike pondered for a few minutes about the things that made him anxious: work stuff, home, money, health, terrorism. He realised he had never really brought these things to God and that he hadn't expected God to help. The words of the preacher came back to him, and something about Jesus saying not to be anxious for the future. It felt odd to speak to God in the office; God was for church. He looked about him embarrassedly as if his colleagues, all preparing to start work and chatting amongst themselves, knew what he was thinking, but he felt drawn to think of Jesus present in the office with him. He imagined himself telling Jesus about his worries and, in a deep sigh, he sensed himself asking for help to cope with the day ahead.

Pause for thought

What are your worries and concerns for the world, your family, your place of work or learning?

Reflection

Mark's Gospel gives a picture of Jesus getting up early and going to a deserted place to pray. Many of us can't contemplate the thought of setting the alarm any earlier than we already do, but perhaps there are ways we can build in a more conscious engagement with God. Even if we have seriously busy mornings we can still probably find ways in which we can connect with God. Mike has almost an hour on his train: how could he use this? Perhaps he could be more conscious about the way he makes use of that 20 minutes in his office at his desk before work begins?

One of the most important things to try to find is some quiet space for God. That might be just about switching off the radio for a period to have some reflection time. It may be about making better use of something which is already part of our morning routine. Perhaps Patrick's story might inspire us.

Patrick catches the train each morning to the school where he's a teacher. He usually spends the train journey reading, but when he gets to the station there is a further journey to make. The school is up a long hill, and there are fairly regular buses up it (usually full of students). When he first started working there, he quickly found that the 20 minutes it took to walk up the hill wasn't much slower than taking a bus – and it provided a great time for some silence and reflection. Patrick wouldn't say he thinks particularly profound thoughts during that time, but he and that hill have become great friends: it helps him gear up for the day as he walks up it each morning and helps him to wind down as he descends it at the end of the day.

As well as getting some space in the morning, it's good to spend some time meditating on the Bible in a way which sets us up for the day. One particular technique which may be helpful is *Lectio Divina*, which is associated with the Benedictine spiritual tradition. It is a way of reading the Bible and praying which involves four stages, though we've found it more helpful to divide them into six. We can try doing these wherever we are.

The first thing we need to do is *prepare*; we need to be intentional about how we are going to use our time in reading the Bible and praying. This means that we should decide where it will take place and how much time we are able to set aside for it. Some of us may have a space in our home where we will be uninterrupted and perhaps we can get up a little earlier to pray. For others it may be about fitting it in to another part of our day – for example, by using part of a journey, as Mike had the opportunity to do. Teachers of the practice of *Lectio Divina* suggest that we should find a quiet place where we won't be distracted for a chosen period of time. Many of us, of course, don't have the luxury of much quiet time or space in our lives to do that, so why not try it on the train or the bus or the tube – or wherever you can? And if you don't have much time, do a bit: a quick 'hello' to God is better than nothing at all! Perhaps the most important part of our preparation is to assess where we are in our relationship with God and what sort of mood we are in. The whole point of this exercise is to bring us closer to God, so it is good to reflect before we begin on where we are at the start.

The next stage is to *read* a particular passage we've chosen from Scripture. It doesn't need to be long – in fact, it's better if it's short. We read it slowly and go over it a few times, paying attention to anything which particularly strikes us. Of course, the Bible is a huge collection of books, so how are we supposed to know where to start? It can be a good idea to follow some kind of scheme. Some people may already use Bible notes; using *Lectio Divina* with the selected passages may provide an excellent way of deepening the time of prayer. Others may follow the pattern of the lectionary, or choose their own reading scheme – for example, by working through a Gospel or one of Paul's letters.

Once we have read the text we *meditate* on the words, chewing them over and pondering them. It may be that certain thoughts and questions arise as we do this, and this can cause us to reflect on the passage far more deeply.

We then begin to *pray*. It may be that we pray in thanksgiving or praise to God, or we may wish to express regret for something that has gone wrong, or perhaps we feel led to pray for a situation of a friend or colleague who is on our heart.

Gradually we let words fail and we have a time of just *being* in God's presence, of letting God love us. The key here is trying to connect with God, rather than learning about the Bible. We're trying to listen to what God is saying *to us*, and perhaps it's something which will keep coming back to us during our working day.

At the end of our time of *Lectio Divina*, even if we've only had a short space, we are in a position to *reassess* where we are with God and how our mood is different. It has been a time of encounter with God and, therefore, we assess at the end how our encounter with God has affected us. We might like to consider what we will take with us from the time of prayer into the day that lies ahead.

Questions for personal reflection or group discussion

- How could you make more space for more time with God in the mornings?

- Do you use anything like *Lectio Divina* at the moment? If not, could you make time for it?

- Do you believe that God wants to communicate with you each day and cares about all that's going on with you?

- Where is your 'desert place'?

Suggested group activity

Try a version of *Lectio Divina* as a group exercise. You will need to choose a passage of Scripture to meditate on.

- Take a few moments to pause and remind yourselves of God's presence. Note inwardly how you are feeling about God, about yourself and about life in general. This is the *preparation* stage.

- Someone reads aloud and slowly the chosen passage of Scripture. Pause for a few minutes, while each of you chews over what you've heard. Then repeat this twice more. This is all part of the *reading* stage; in it we're trying to allow the words to speak to us.

- Next comes the *meditation* stage. Spend some time either sharing with others anything which has resonated with you, or you might each do this in silence.

- Then, spend some time in either open corporate prayer or quiet individual prayer. Agree before you begin how long this should be.

- Allow words to fail for some time as a group, and rest together in God's presence for some minutes.

- Finally, have a time of review together as a group; discuss how the encounter changed your mood, your outlook or anything which you've particularly noticed.

Suggestions for prayer

It's Tuesday, Lord, and my mind is full of things
I have to do,
worries, concerns, anxieties . . .
I can't stop my head buzzing!
Help me to find the space to gaze on you,
to get a moment or two of stillness,
and receive the peace I need.
I ask this through Jesus Christ our Lord.
Amen.

A prayer at the beginning of a working day (the hour of Terce, the third hour)

Lord,
like your good friend Martha,
we must be busy now with many things.

Help us also to attend upon you;
to listen to you,
like your good friend Mary,
and so to hear your voice
amid the noise and clamour of activities
taken up in your name.
Amen.

Wednesday

'Whatever your task, put yourselves into it, as done for the Lord and not for your masters, since you know that from the Lord you will receive the inheritance as your reward; you serve the Lord Christ.'

Colossians 3:23-24

Wednesday is right in the middle of the week, so it can seem like the most ordinary day. But the weekend is now in sight! By Wednesday evening we can feel as though we've 'broken the back of the week'. Here we explore possibilities for engaging with God in both the middle of the week and the middle of the day. In Christian spiritual tradition, prayer in the middle of the day is known as 'Sext' (at the sixth hour).

Teresa's story

'Which lunch break do you want, Teresa?' asked her supervisor. 'Early, please,' Teresa replied. Early lunch meant that Teresa could slip into St Augustine's Church round the corner from the store where she worked. There was Mass there every day at 12.15pm. She really valued meeting with God in the Eucharist not just on Sundays but also a couple of times in the week. On other days she might opt for a later lunch when St Augustine's would be still and quiet and she could spend 15 or 20 minutes in silent prayer or meditation. The store was always busy and, even when there were fewer customers, there was always stock to check in or clothes to fold or hang back on rails. Teresa would be on her feet all day and so this brief respite in the day was very welcome. Whilst she sat quietly in the church she liked to choose a story from the Gospels and imagine herself in it, letting God speak to her through it. She did not feel obliged to say any prayers. It was enough to be in the presence of God, especially in such an ancient place where so many people had prayed before her.

Back at the store her colleagues imagined she was meeting someone special: a lovers' tryst! One day they told her what they thought she was up to in her lunch breaks. She told them they were correct: it was a lovers' tryst of sorts. Then she told them about her visits to the church. Somehow they weren't surprised. 'Next time,' her supervisor quipped, 'say one for me!' 'I will, of course,' responded Teresa with her usual cheeriness, before she turned to serve her next customer.

Pause for thought

What opportunities during the day do you have to engage with God?

Reflection

One of the challenges of trying to live out our faith 'seven whole days' is finding ways of engaging with God throughout an ordinary day, especially when we get busy. How can we 'catch God's eye' as we go about our mundane / stressful / exciting / consuming / relentless (delete as appropriate!) business? Or is it perhaps a case of letting *our* eyes be caught by God?

In our story, Teresa finds that slipping out to St Augustine's during her lunch break re-centres her with God, enabling her to find God in the work she does. On some days it is a service of Holy Communion which provides the nourishment; on others it is the quiet time of her own prayers and meditations. What might sustain us spiritually in an average day?

Some of us would love the idea of some silence or a Eucharist in the middle of the day, but don't have the option. Is it still possible to find God throughout the day, even if we don't get a single minute to ourselves? Crucially, we need to remember that God is everywhere: his presence is with us wherever we are.

In his Rule, St Benedict taught his monks this: 'Hour by hour keep careful watch over all you do, aware that God's gaze is upon you, wherever you may be'.[11] The Rule covers every aspect of life, making no distinctions between the sacred and the secular. You find instructions on everything from obedience and reverence in prayer right through to daily manual labour and the sleeping arrangements of the monks. All parts of life are considered service to God. The cellarer (the monk who looks after the monastery's supplies) is told to 'regard all utensils and goods of the monastery as sacred vessels of the altar'.[12]

This can help us to see our ordinary routine life as our service of God. Think of those slaves St Paul was speaking to in the passage from Colossians: they didn't have the freedom to change what they were doing, but they *did* have the freedom to serve God *in and through* their work. That is why

---

11. RB 4.48-49.
12. RB 31.10.

Paul tells them to think of themselves doing it *for God* and not their masters.

How does this challenge the way we approach the ordinary things we have to do on a day-to-day basis? Do we consider the laptop, the paintbrush, the work desk, the screwdriver, the mobile phone as 'sacred vessels of the altar'?

The Ignatian spiritual tradition, based on the teachings of St Ignatius of Loyola (1491–1556), Founder of the Society of Jesus (Jesuits), is extremely useful in providing techniques to find God in all things. Indeed, Jesuits are often thought of as being 'contemplatives in action', fully engaged in the world whilst remaining firmly committed to prayer and meditation. One particular technique they espouse is *imaginative contemplation,* which works particularly well for stories from the Gospels about Jesus. This is a way of seeking to meet God through the use of our imagination in which we can enter more fully into a story from the Scriptures and address our concerns to God in prayer, before 'bathing' in his presence.

As we saw with *Lectio Divina* on Tuesday, it is important to spend time preparing practically for this sort of exercise and reflecting on where we are with God before we begin.

We begin by reading a story from the Bible, perhaps a miracle story or one in which Jesus is being compassionate to someone in need. We then close our eyes and imagine the scene: imagine the sights, the smells, the feel of the hot air, the sounds around us . . . and then we play the Gospel scene out in our mind's eye. We watch the reactions on the faces of those we can see; we hear the words Jesus says; perhaps we even become a character in the scene.

Once it is played out in our mind we come to Jesus ourselves (it doesn't matter if we can't fully imagine what he looks like) and have a chat with him. We share with him what's on our heart, talking with him as a friend and sharing our concerns, for example: 'Jesus, I have a particularly difficult day ahead today. I'm really struggling with that project I'm working on and I don't know what to do. I'm also nervous about seeing Jenny and don't want to get into another argument. Can you help me to love Andrew more and not feel so angry?'

As with *Lectio Divina*, we can then let our words come to an end and rest ourselves in the presence of Christ, allowing God to love us. When this time of prayer draws to a close, we can also spend time assessing what impact it has had on us and reflecting on what we can take from it into the day ahead. Perhaps Teresa, in her imagination, brings before God all that's been going on in her day. As she does so, she can see more clearly where to find God in the midst of it and she returns to work with renewed energy. She can find God in the middle of an ordinary and mundane Wednesday!

Questions for personal reflection or group discussion

- How can we remind ourselves that God is always with us?

- Do you see your ordinary routine as service of God?

- What do you think of the idea that ordinary, everyday items could be like 'sacred vessels' of the altar? What does that mean for you?

Suggested group activity

Try a version of imaginative contemplation as a group exercise. Someone will need to read out this meditation, based upon Luke 17:11-19.

Make yourself comfortable, close your eyes and come before God in an attitude of prayer. I want you to imagine a village at the time of Jesus – and imagine that you're standing in the village. Look around at the houses and other buildings you see around you; feel the heat of the day on your skin; smell the smells in the air; hear the sounds of the village and the surrounding wildlife. Take a few moments to savour the scene.

And now imagine in the village a group of ten people. Notice that they are lepers: look at the clothes they are wearing; consider how their skin looks; see the expressions on their faces; watch them engage with one another.

And now you see Jesus enter the village . . . Observe their reactions to him. Watch as they begin to approach Jesus. But as they are lepers they are not allowed to come into contact with other people. Observe the way they keep their distance.

They begin to shout out, saying, 'Jesus, Master, have mercy on us!' Hear them do this and observe their faces . . .

Then Jesus speaks to them: 'Go and show yourselves to the priests.' Watch them all as they turn to go and do as he asks. Then observe how as they walk away they become clean; see their skin changed as the leprosy is healed. And watch them as they continue to walk away.

Then observe one of them turn back. See the expression on his face. Watch him as he praises God with a loud voice . . . And now he prostrates himself at Jesus' feet . . . and hear him utter words of thanksgiving.

Now turn your attention back to Jesus. He looks at the man. And he says these words: 'Were not ten made clean? But the other nine, where are they? Was none of them found to return and give praise to God except you?' Then he says: 'Get up and go on your way; your faith has saved you.'

Take a few moments to be in Christ's presence, to say a few words to him in your imagination, if you like . . . And finally allow the scene to draw to a close – and we come back together as a group.

Suggestions for prayer

On Wednesday, Lord,
the end of the week is in sight,
but there's still so much to do!
Help me in whatever I'm doing
to find some space for you.
Amen.

A prayer for the middle of the day
(the hour of Sext, the sixth hour of the day)

Lord,
you have called us to labour in the vineyard
of your kingdom.
Help us, in the noontime of our endeavours,
to know when to work on
and when to stop for rest and refreshment;
for your name's sake.
Amen.

Thursday

"Then he led them out as far as Bethany, and, lifting up his hands, he blessed them. While he was blessing them, he withdrew from them and was carried up into heaven.'

Luke 24:50-51

Thursday is the day on which the Church celebrates the Ascension of Christ to heaven. On this feast we remind ourselves of the glory and reign of Christ, but we also reflect on the fact that we're still here on earth awaiting the final coming of the kingdom of God. We might have glimpses of glory on a Thursday – after all, the weekend isn't far away! – but although Christ is ascended to the right hand of the Father, we are left on earth in the messiness of everyday life. Thursday is a day to 'keep on keeping on'. How can we spot the glory of the ascended Christ in our mundane reality?

It is the afternoon. In Christian spiritual tradition, prayer in the afternoon is called None or Nones (pronounced like 'known') and relates to the ninth hour of the day or 3pm.

Barry's story

Barry took the opportunity, between shifts, to take the family car to be serviced. As it was to take only an hour and a half, Barry decided to wait at the garage. The small waiting room was comfortable enough and the hot drinks machine looked inviting. Barry soon became bored reading the advertisements that decorated the walls. The 'auto' magazines did not appeal to him. He settled for playing Sudoku on his mobile phone.

Two women came into the waiting room. Barry supposed them to be mother and daughter. They chatted about this and that. What might be wrong with the car? Whom had they seen lately? Then they took to discussing the grandmother of the family who had been diagnosed with Alzheimer's disease. The conversation changed in colour and tone as they chortled about some of the things she says. They lowered their voices to a whisper when speaking of the grandmother's personal care needs. Barry heard every word. After a short while they were called back to reception and, soon after, he saw them drive away.

Barry thanked the Lord they had gone! He sensed the Lord give him a cautionary look and so prayed for the two women and for the grandmother in all her needs. He prayed for the family as they sought to cope. He prayed for the doctor's surgery staff in their busy day (the woman had been having difficulty getting an appointment). He found himself praying for his own family and others whose needs were on his heart. He prayed for the garage staff and thanked God for the luxury of a reliable car and for his work, to which he must return by three o'clock. Just then the receptionist called him through. All was well.

Pause for thought

Are there ways in which you relate to Barry's story?

Reflection

An interesting passage from the Rule of St Benedict gives us a clue as to how we might find God, as Barry does, in the ordinary reality of everyday life:

Obedience will be acceptable to God and pleasing to all only if what is commanded is done without hesitation, delay, lukewarmness, grumbling, or objection. For if the disciple obeys with an ill will and murmurs, not necessarily with his lips but simply in his heart, then even though he fulfil the command yet his work will not be acceptable to God, who sees that his heart is murmuring.[13]

Though we're sure few readers are living a monastic life in a religious order, we think we can all learn something from St Benedict's approach. He's not talking about blind obedience to an unjust authority, but rather about our attitude to what's happening in our lives. Like Barry, many of us are having to get on with the mundane tasks of life, like waiting for our car to be serviced.

We can't be a human being without facing the fact that life involves getting on with things we'd rather not do. It might be anything: walking the dog, attending meetings we're committed to, visiting family, turning up to fulfil our duties at church, looking after the children, writing a report for the boss, hanging out the washing, going into work . . . The list goes on. The attitude with which we approach these tasks is crucial: we can do them all with a grumble in our hearts, or

---

13. RB 5.14.

we can try to find God in them. St Benedict's insight is that obedience is only worthwhile if we've got the right attitude.

Of course, there are times when it would be wrong for us to be obedient. Perhaps we may need to stand up against a situation of injustice in our workplace. It's absolutely right that we are called to be salt and light in the world, to maintain high ethical standards, but in those circumstances our response should be carefully considered *protest* rather than murmuring or grumbling. When we oppose injustice or stand up for an ethical perspective, this should be done with the virtues of Christ: humility, kindness, meekness.

After Barry notes the Lord's 'cautionary look', his attitude towards the whole situation was changes. Instead of feeling bored and irritated by those around him, he turns to prayer. In particular, he prays for others: *intercession*. As we think of ourselves as those who are 'left on earth' after the Ascension, we also need to remember that Christ 'entered into heaven itself, now to appear in the presence of God on our behalf' (Hebrews 9:24). The Ascension reminds us that Christ is interceding on our behalf, and like him we should intercede on behalf of others. Intercession changes Barry's whole attitude: he ceases to be bored and irritated. In thinking about the needs of others in prayer, he realises the blessings in his own life. Barry catches a glimpse of God in the ordinary.

Questions for personal reflection or group discussion

- What sorts of things do we grumble about?

- When do we need to be more obedient? What might that mean in your life?

- Think of occasions when protest is more appropriate than obedience. How should Christians conduct themselves on these occasions?

Suggested group activity

Each person in the group is invited to write down three grumbles they find themselves moaning about often. Then go around the group sharing one of your grumbles. Say whether you could make a resolution to stop grumbling about it and seek the advice of others on how to resolve it.

Suggestions for prayer

It's Thursday, Lord, and I've got a grumble list,
with plenty of gripes and groans.
It doesn't seem fair that Jesus is ascended to heaven
and I'm stuck on earth!
Help me to remember that you're with me here,
praying for me,

help me to catch a glimpse of glory in the ordinary
and mundane,
help me to pray for others, too.
For the sake of your Son, Jesus Christ.
Amen.

A prayer for the middle of the afternoon (the hour of None, the ninth hour of the day)

As the day unfolds, dear Lord,
and we are running late,
and running out of energy,
renew our strength,
lift us up on eagle's wings,
for all that is still to do;
for you are our strength,
our might and our salvation.
Amen.

Friday

'They urged [Jesus] strongly, saying, "Stay with us, because it is almost evening and the day is now nearly over." So he went in to stay with them.'

Luke 24:29

'Thank God that day's over!' 'Thank God it's Friday!'

Do you ever find yourself saying these things? We certainly do! Surely everyone loves that 'Friday feeling'. Whether or not it's actually Friday, the end of a day or a busy working week is a special time. The end of a period of work and into rest is indeed a time to give thanks to God. Friday is also the day of the crucifixion of Christ and a day of penance. Just as we looked at beginning the day on Monday and Tuesday, in this chapter we look at how we end the day. In the evening we reflect on all that has been and ask God what we need to carry and what we can lay down; we reflect on the things over which we need to express sorrow and the blessings for which we might give thanks.

Danny's story

Danny was reluctant to go home that evening. He had flounced out of the house just after lunch because his mother had packed him off to the Job Centre to see what he could find. He was very angry with her because he had been down there three times already that week. He had been all over the city since then (or at least that is how it felt), chasing possibilities. The first place he went to, the vacancy had been filled but they had forgotten to tell the Job Centre. The second place had given him forms to fill out and spoken of training on the job and prospects, but he would have to return for a formal interview and they would need to take up references.

The third place had closed for the weekend. Tired, angry and despondent, he made his way slowly home, wondering how he was going to face his Mum after the way he had been so rude to her earlier.

As he trudged home, he passed a poster on a church notice-board which read: 'Bad Friday or Good Friday?'

Danny began to reflect on the day. It had started well (though not early!) with catching up with friends on a social media site: most of them from the church youth group. Whilst out at the shops, someone whom he admired very much had returned his smile. Egg and chips for lunch and then . . . the row. Danny reflected on the afternoon. The people at the second place were nice to him and seemed keen for him to pursue his application. Shame about the wasted time and energy on the other two. Danny remembered the curate at church saying something about weighing up the good and the bad, so that the bad did not make you lose sight of the good. On reflection, the day had not been all bad.

Danny opened the door cautiously. 'I'm home, Mum.' 'There you are, Danny. Get your coat off. I'll put the kettle on. Now, how did you get on?' 'Sorry about earlier,' he said.

Pause for thought

What strikes you about the way Danny reviews his day?

Reflection

So often we don't give ourselves enough time for reflection and thanksgiving. In the same way as making time to praise God early in the morning, making space for gratitude in the evening is a habit to cultivate. It's one which has huge benefits. It's all too tempting to finish one thing and then rush off into the next without giving ourselves a breather – but often a breather is exactly what we need! We might wish to ease straight into rest at the end of a busy period and forget all about the past week (or indeed get straight into the host of other jobs which have to be done at home!), but it's worth pausing to take stock, expressing both sorrow and gratitude for the time which has passed.

One way of getting such reflection is to use the prayer of the *Examen*, a prayer-filled exercise St Ignatius taught his followers to do twice daily. It's this sort of thing which Danny finds himself doing as he trudges home after a seemingly 'Bad Friday'. Just as with some of the ways we've explored for praying in the morning, the *Examen* can be done anywhere: in silence with a candle in a room on your own, or on the bus, the tube, the train, or as you are walking about. The point of this exercise is to review in the presence of God the day that has passed.

The exercise begins with taking time to be still and to remember that we are always in God's presence. We then ask for God's light as we review the period of time we've chosen to look at. Next, we begin to recall the events of the chosen time period, allowing memories and feelings and moods to come to mind.

In doing this, certain things will enter our consciousness which we don't feel so good about, which seem drained of light and energy: a difficult conversation we had; a problem we were working on; a feeling of frustration or boredom. Other moments will feel good, full of light and happiness: perhaps simply the taste of our lunch or a cup of coffee; the smile of a friend; the moment when we were in the sunshine for a second.

As we come towards the end of this time of prayerful reflection, we ask for God's light for those more difficult bits of the chosen period of time, and perhaps we need to say sorry to God for neglecting his presence in those moments. We also give thanks to God for the blessings we've had that day, for his presence through those good things we've enjoyed. Like Danny, we might find that our day has not been 'all bad'; often when people use this prayer they find themselves surprised at some of the memories which occur, moments of happiness they'd completely forgotten about.

This prayer is all about giving us a chance to reflect on where God has been present throughout the day, even if we haven't noticed it. Often we will discover that we found God in those things for which we are now giving thanks: that he was with us all the time, and yet we missed him! As we pray the *Examen* more frequently, we might gradually start to think at certain moments in the day, 'Ah, I'm going to give thanks to God for this later!' This is exactly the point at which to stop and notice that *God is with you now*. We may also notice those behaviours and attitudes which don't bring us closer to God, which drain the light and energy from us. Gradually we can become more aware of these things and try to amend them with the help of the Holy Spirit.

In the story of the road to Emmaus the two disciples urge Jesus to stay with them, because it is almost evening and the day is nearly over. This, of course, is exactly what we are trying to do: urge Christ to continue to be with us – and how willing he is to do as we ask!

Questions for personal reflection or group discussion

- Reflect on your experience of the 'Friday feeling'.

- How can we make time to pause and reflect in gratitude and sorrow?

- Is there someone towards whom you need to make a gesture of reconciliation?

Suggested group activity

Try a version of the *Examen* as a group exercise. Someone will need to read out this meditation.

Make yourself comfortable, perhaps close your eyes, and do whatever you can to find some stillness . . . Maybe focus on your breathing, breathing in God's love, breathing out the concerns of the day – and continue to do this for a few moments . . .

Know that you are surrounded by God's love and always in his presence . . . And now ask God to give you his light as you review your day . . .

Then gradually cast your mind back over moments of the day today, recalling in particular the things for which you are grateful and anything you particularly regret . . . Perhaps a conversation with a friend, something you ate, some task you achieved . . . Spend a couple of minutes in this silent recollection . . . And now give thanks to God for the gifts he has given to you, thanking him for those moments when he was present – even if you didn't recognise it . . . And take a moment to express your sorrow for anything that went wrong.

Finally, we draw our prayers to a close.

Suggestions for prayer

Oh God, I'm tired! Thank God it's Friday . . .
But help me pause a while.
There's so much that's happened today,
so help me to find a chance to say 'sorry' and 'thanks',

to notice where you've been with me all along,
even though I didn't notice you.
I make this prayer though Jesus Christ.
Amen.

A prayer for early evening (the hour of Vespers)

Be with us, Lord,
as we journey home,
mindful of being reunited with home, family, friends,
or returning to isolation and solitude.
Teach us to live in hope all our days
and grace us with the knowledge
of your abiding presence with us.
Amen.

Saturday

'A great gale arose, and the waves beat into the boat, so that the boat was already being swamped. But [Jesus] was in the stern, asleep on the cushion.'

Mark 4:37-38

As we learnt on Sunday, *Saturday* is the original Sabbath, the day of rest. For many people Saturday is a day on which to recover from the stresses of the week. In this final session we reflect on the importance of rest for the spiritual life and explore how we might find God in and through resting.

Jackie's story

Jackie never minded working on Saturday nights. Unless there was an emergency admission her hospital ward would be relatively quiet. Most of her patients would have had surgery earlier in the week and would now be recovering and, more than anything, they needed sleep through the hours of night.

As the day nurse completed her 'handover' report, she picked up her bag and parted from Jackie with the words: 'All is well, Jackie – have a good night.'

Jackie made her first round of the patients, greeting them quietly; some of them were already sleepy. She came to an elderly man whose prognosis was poor. He had been a Christian minister in his time. In spite of serious difficulties, he always managed a smile and would ask Jackie how she was and if she had slept well during the day. Tonight, however, he was very low. His wife was at his side and was reading to him the ancient office of Compline or 'night prayer'. Jackie recognised it from church. The church council said it together sometimes and it was used in church at certain times of the year, such as late evening in Lent or Advent. She had always found that its gentle cadences had a calming and reassuring effect on her and brought her a comforting sense of the presence of God.

As Jackie gently adjusted the man's pillows, his wife was reading: 'We will lay us down in peace and take our rest; for it is thou, Lord, only, that makest us dwell in safety.'[14] To be honest, Jackie could just do with laying herself down and taking her rest. It was her fourth night on duty in a row and she hadn't been sleeping well during the day, but she knew her strength would be renewed once she had rested properly.

The elderly minister's life ebbed peacefully away during the night. He would not see the dawn of Sunday morning, but Jackie did, and she gave thanks to God for it, for the life and witness of her patient, for a few days' rest and for the new week ahead.

Pause for thought

What connections do you make between falling asleep, dying and resting in God's hands?

Reflection

In the story Jackie notices how beautifully the office of Compline helps us to let ourselves go into the presence of

---

14. See http://www.oremus.org/liturgy/ireland/compline.html

God. Compline, or some other form of 'night prayer', is a great way to end the day, when we can manage it. It's a very short service which we can do on our own or in a group before going to bed. The word 'compline' comes from the Latin *completorium*, meaning 'completion'; it gives us the chance to place everything into God's hands, knowing that he will hold it while we slip into unconsciousness.[15]

Compline is a service of rest and reflection, which gives us permission to sink into sleep, knowing that the work of the day is done and is now in God's hands. In the words of the *Nunc Dimittis*: 'Now, Lord, you let your servant go in peace: your word has been fulfilled' (Luke 2:29, *Common Worship*).[16] This canticle may be found in many contemporary services of Evening Prayer, evidence that such services are based on a seventeenth-century fusion of the ancient offices of Vespers and Compline.

Sleep is a hugely important gift of God. This may be an unfamiliar concept, but sleep is actually a vital part of our relationship with God. Explicit times of prayer can help frame the day, but they are only one aspect of a deep relationship with God that continues 24 hours a day. In making a commitment to specific prayer times or 'quiet times', we need to be honest with ourselves about how our body clock works and how our household works. We also need to be aware of the

15. See https://www.churchofengland.org/prayer-worship/worship/texts/daily2/night/compline.aspx.
16. See https://www.churchofengland.org/prayer-worship/worship/texts/daily2/canticles/ntcanticles.aspx#56

needs of others and to balance our other responsibilities and obligations. It is worth experimenting with different times of the day for prayer and with the length of time we commit to explicit prayer. Whatever the time of day the prayer begins, it can be considered as sustaining a conversation with God that continues in many verbal and non-verbal forms until the next explicit prayer rendezvous. Arguably, the longest period of a day in which we rest in our relationship with God is when he blesses us with sleep. Receiving his blessing throughout our sleep time is unselfconscious prayer.

As we ask God for the blessed gift of sleep, we might even like to use a conscious form of prayer as we lie in our bed, to help us slip into slumber, especially when we're stressed or going through a particularly difficult time. You might use the imaginative contemplation method we explored on Wednesday, meditating on the story from Mark 4:35-41, as you lie down to sleep. You might wish to imagine that the pillow on your bed is the cushion in the boat with Jesus. (A suggested meditation can be found in the group activity on page 81.)

Some authorities assert that one in three Britons suffers from poor sleep, owing to stress, computers and taking work home. This can result in bad moods and a lack of focus. More seriously, regular poor sleep puts people at risk of developing various medical conditions, including obesity, heart disease and diabetes, and it shortens life expectancy. Perhaps such possibilities might encourage us to get enough sleep.

Sleep is also crucial from a spiritual perspective. One Christian writer suggests that sleep 'is the ultimate act of vulnerability, and of trust that everything does not depend on our own heroic activity'.[17] When we fall asleep we acknowledge that we are mortal, that we can't be conscious all the time, that we must allow the world to fend for itself without our presence. Some people seem to have the attitude that sleep is for wimps, a belief that it is a virtue to be able to cope on four to five hours a night so that they can get more done. However, we believe that sleep is for the brave: those who can trust God, who don't commit the hubris of thinking the world depends on them. We need to let go of the world each night by falling asleep; sleep helps us to put the sense of our own importance into perspective. We are not God, who 'will neither slumber nor sleep', as the Psalmist says (Psalm 121:4). The world can manage jolly well without *us* for seven or eight hours in a 24-hour period, whether our work or our lifestyle causes us to sleep during the hours of night or during the day!

Sleep also reminds us of the God-given need to rest and take time off work. In Psalm 127:2 we read: 'It is in vain that you rise up early and go late to rest, eating the bread of anxious toil; for he gives sleep to his beloved.' The God we believe in is the God who gives us the concept of the Sabbath, the time of rest from our toil. What a contrast this is from the

---

17. Nick Jowett, 'A theology of slumber', *Church Times*, 14 February 2014.

philosophy of the busy world which surrounds us! With our smartphones we can now be logged into work anywhere or any time we choose; this can be very unhealthy and prevents us from the need we all have to switch off from work. Taking rest reminds us that work is *part* of life, not its sum total. It reminds us that we are created by God for joy. Taking rest also helps us to work more effectively and prevents burnout.

The story is told that St Anthony of the Desert (c.251–356) was relaxing with his disciples outside his hut when a hunter came by. The hunter was surprised to see Anthony relaxing, and rebuked him for taking it easy. It wasn't his idea of what a holy monk should be doing!

Anthony replied, 'Bend your bow and shoot an arrow.' The hunter did so. 'Bend it again and shoot another arrow.' The hunter did so again, and again and again, as Anthony commanded.

Finally, the hunter said, 'Abba Anthony, if I keep my bow always stretched it will break.'

'So it is with the monk,' said Anthony. 'If we push ourselves beyond measure, we will break. It is right from time to time to relax from our efforts.'

Rest can remind us of exactly what is important in life. Few people as they die express the wish that they'd spent more time at the office!

Questions for personal reflection or group discussion

- Do you see sleep as part of your relationship with God? Why might this be difficult for some people to accept?

- What lessons can we learn from the need for sleep?

- Reflect on the balance in your own life between work, rest, fun, sleep, etc.

Suggested group activity

Try a version of this imaginative contemplation as a group exercise. Someone will need to read out this meditation, slowly and reflectively.

Make yourself comfortable, close your eyes and come before God in an attitude of prayer . . .

Imagine that you are in a boat with Jesus and the disciples on the Sea of Galilee . . . Night has fallen and as you strain at the oars a great gale blows up. The waves beat against the boat, and water pours in over the sides. Feel the impact of the wind and waves; feel the cold, wet rain on your skin; feel the motion of the boat, moving up and down on the waves; notice the faces of the other disciples as they strain against the oars . . .

Consider all of your stresses and concerns; imagine that they are those angry waves which are threatening you, preventing you from resting . . .

Now see Jesus. He is asleep on a cushion in the stern of the boat . . . As you look at him fast asleep, consider his great trust in God, how he is able to let himself go into God's loving arms . . .

Now imagine that you are putting your oar down and go to Jesus . . . Lie down next to him; try to get a sense of his rest and his trust in God . . . Then notice the other disciples waking Jesus up: 'Teacher, do you not care that we are perishing?' they say.

You continue to lie down, but are aware that Jesus is standing up, saying to the wind and the sea: 'Peace! Be still!' He says these words to you, too . . . He is in control. . . You do not need to be concerned about anything . . .

As the wind and waves begin to calm in your imagination, allow your anxieties and concerns to slip away with them . . . God is holding them. You can rest.

Suggestions for prayer

Lord, your servant Simeon was content to depart in peace.
Help me to trust in you.
As I fall asleep, may I rest in your presence.
As I slumber, may I trust in you, that you've got
everything covered.
As I rest, may I continue to pray, even though
I don't know it.

And when I awake, may I be refreshed and ready
to serve you.
For the love of Jesus Christ, your Son.
Amen.

A prayer at the end of the day
(the hour of Compline, night prayer)

O Lord,
as we come to the end of this day,
we recall your Son laid to rest in the
Garden of the Sepulchre.
At this late hour we offer ourselves,
and all your people,
into your safe keeping,
knowing that you are always with us,
and in joyful anticipation of encountering you again
in the morning
in the Garden of the Resurrection of your same Son,
our Lord Jesus Christ.
Amen.